Battered

yet

Beautiful

By Leija Farr

A Young Urban Author Publication

Copyright © 2013 Leija Farr

Cover Design: Fusion Creative Works

Developmental Editor: Frankie Roe

Publisher: Young Urban Authors

www.youngurbanauthors.org

ISBN-13:978-1493742219

ISBN-10:1493742213

Library of Congress Control Number (applied for)

Dedication

I dedicate this poem to my family. I also dedicate it to my future children since they may read this.

R.I.P Baba

Bars

They tell him he got, bars.

Drenching lips in fictional stories he's never lived,
spitting lines of hurt he has never been black and
blue'd with, but they tell him he got, bars.

He clothes skin with stories he sees on the news,
wraps the mind in things he reads about, letting the
print print his body in fairytales.

He raps about lives his pupils see on corners, letting
his mouth be the umbilical cord of their blooming
stories, plagiarizing pain and broadcasting as his
own.

Impregnating thoughts with reality, he births them,
pushing them out on microphones, claiming cold
streets raised him, remixing the texture of homes
where broken dreams scatter grounds, stabbing
hope. He rhymes like those hard times he visualized
in mirrors, like his shoes walk beside shadows on
the blocks with liquor stores, storing a father's
addiction.

He bodies his opponents, but bodies with scars
staining masterpieces he never mentions screaming
"I sold drugs and got shot" telling another's diary
the lethal mix of sensation and shell cases.

He talks a dented truth, tongue kissing wind with
the ink of someone else's metaphors and similes, he
turns horror simple but seeing bloody images soak
brain cells can never equal simplicity.

And what he tries to build is far from what can be
constructed, he tries on the attire of someone's
stones building a heart to keep it from being torn,
seeing examples of rappers turning struggle exciting
but the sight of the truth leaves faces erect
recognizing the pudding really holds the proof and
it's not appetizing

But he swallows their dishes like life allowed him
to see them be grilled, seeing streets that fry and
sometimes are too burnt to be adored. They say he
got bars when he's taking incarceration, speaking
their shackles, claiming blood he never leaked.

Painted World

Carve on blank canvases beauty flourishing from withered corners, scar buildings with the images developing in the mind's lens. Let's shade sidewalks with sweet thoughts, painting sugar coated dreams we carry but never birth. This world where we place pastels to starving alleyways, color sparkle in the eyes of torn toddlers so the world seems brighter. Let's paint this world. Because me and you have brushes that can make masterpieces of broken pieces, loving what once stabbed us.

~~Perfection~~

Don't let anyone tell you that your god-painted
beauty is not perfection. Perfection is not real.
Though models try to show us normalcy and boys
try to intoxicate us with potent lies, perfection is
extinct in the structure of mirrors, no reflection has
ever stained the words perfection on fragile glass.

The loads of makeup we consume to make up
flawlessness, the times we cry on pillows because
life told us tears shade shadows I tell you to lift up
your head and see the rainbows.

Wars we go through for hourglass figures and feel
ashamed when figures can't fit in jeans. I tell you to
ignore what people told you perfection was.
Perfection is not real. So rather than swallow those
lies, dissect those same mirrors people tell you
perfection lives in, and carve your own definition.

Lip Stained Boys

I see the boys.
With the lipstick stains, blooming cherry scents on
cheeks. They bare the lipstick stains of hurt
mothers. Who feared that this world would twist
their silhouettes into sour definitions of men. Who
wished they could beautify the same streets they
drowned in as little boys, swimming in nighttime
tragedy.

Battered by jewelry, there is a confused mind, with
pupils picking up puzzle pieces. They live in a
world, badly broken, as they search corners for role
models so tempted to follow in the footsteps of
shoes barely there.

These boys wear the same lipstick that went through
wearing tears as makeup. Carving their soles
against cold corners, but not carved deep enough
inside them was the word love, lynched in shadows,
the definition's aroma lingers on their tongue but
could never stick and be tasted.

I look at him and see his mother's lipstick stains.
She hopes and hopes and hopes. That if the streets

11

murder him, the lipstick stain sitting along his cheek, will show a mother who never stopped loving.

Silence

Silence . If dissected, the loudest roar may live in it's shadows.

Showers

In life you will have showers but remember rainbows will come soon after

Untitled

Deep in his eyes, you see a shallow soul. With limbs careless enough to abandon his creations he splattered in the blank canvas of a woman.

Imprisoning a child's minds in questions heard from their raisin dried tongues. He starved their dreams, craving drenched images, living but through mirrors they seem lifeless.

Pounding pavements with the hurt of daddy's ghost portraits. He abused their skin without touching them, the pain he painted when he left footprints at the hospital they bloomed from could imprint more bruises than knuckles could.

Mommy's words could never print his voice in their ears, at nighttime they get intoxicated in images they think of him. Heartless. Coward. Donor. Dipped in a deadbeat father's existence, blown away with the wind.

Children need mothers as much as fathers, but fathers turn sperm donors, kids grow to know that daddy could never see the beauty he crafted, his

disappearance penetrated a mother's heart,
connecting to his child's fingers, so when they pick
up pens to write about him the led leaks the same
capacity of blood they cut out of them.

Cutting became the norm of nights when drugs
couldn't get them high enough to leave life behind
them. Deep in his eyes there is a shallow soul, as
shallow as his look at what a father is.

Drawing

He draws like his life depends on it. Shapes he buries in sketch pads, building images constructed by fingers, led kissing sweet liquids on paper because drawing is his first love.

Embedded in the mind, he wears art like clothes, oozing through his fingers finding home in the form of sculptures. He is a boy defined by the lines and curves sunk on sheets for memory. He is defined by his thoughts boiling in pens and scrambled before pupils, eyeing what he lives for, paintings turned mind pixels absorbed and made permanent he draws because words can't reach everywhere in this world he feels alone, cold corners hold his secrets but canvases created new silence.

His silence that births beauty in beaten eyes, he is drawing because beaten eyes need to heal and his models work like magic to people waiting for God's arms to touch them. He draws like he's putting every ounce of hurt and blood and lungs and a throat turned coward into his creations.

He never really had a voice but his pictures have a pitch roars couldn't copy and paste, penetrating notebooks like he just needs someone to hug, to be there when laughter turns ghosts and love translucent.

With his pen, sky isn't the limit, his hands swirl limitless as he shows the world that words can be simplified. And creates a story that only the eyes will consume.

GUN

G-U-N. Letters carved across your black ashed fingers. What started as a toy from daddy's bottom drawer but it was not enough. One shot was not enough to satisfy your gun high, you realized your nose loved the smell of this lethal smoke fuming from bullet holes. Because you saw rappers molest imaginary pistols in songs and misuse bullets and spray homicidal rainbows on pavement.

You decided to put the most focus on this small silhouette that housed in pockets, looked beautiful to you because it is silver painted but as soon as it's penetrated fades to an evil black.

Wanted to use guns as self-defense, you wear weak in school so you would hold it and pray with eyes tightly closed it molded into your skin. And you loved the way people ran when you hit lead into crying pigment, you didn't listen when they told you guns were no fun.

You just repeatedly raped it and made handguns forcefully cum bullets, you blasted big caves in faces, letting dented metal secrete through the peak of the gun hole like liquid let your index inject into rifles despite seeing babies you see sprayed.

Left the taste of sour from the gunpowder you fed to innocent mouths and overtime you curved burns onto knuckles but just chuckled. This was funny to you. That you were holding something so deadly you see the police beat black and blue every day, you see music videos portrayed with glamorized shell cases street corners turn from normal days to loud bangs, when you're were little tried to cover ears with hands smeared with gun art and now it's become you.

You've become the one with the fast reaction to pick up this gun and blast, never really caring how scary this weapon you were holding was. But your eardrums need to hear the sound POP,POP,POP,POP, a sensation for some reason you loved. In movies you see it's cool so you think it's cool to make bodies crawl and lay on them your horrific art of stroking bodies red, and in this time in your life you felt dead and like nobody so you wondered,"why can't everybody else be.

Your fingers swallowed tears strolled down cheeks as you shot this glock, you couldn't stop because you were drunk of this generation's lies, you were drunk off bars emcee's feed to you, you were drunk off Tv's meaning of a thug, took shots of the evil liquid life gives you then eyes became tipsy and would see whatever blurry visions the media gave to you.

You shot so many times that overtime your hands couldn't feel it anymore. Numb to what runs out the gun's mouth and is dug into innocent flesh. Your body has become one with this machine because you can't seem to walk away.

You can't seem to walk into places and not strike it with violent rage can't communicate with your mouth, so you reload your only focus and hope and shoot it. You're wondering why the gun never answers your cries? Because gun's are not your friends. It doesn't care who's dead it's brian is just a blank structure that shoots whatever, it just cares it's getting fame from every person that plays with it.

That it's shape is being bedazzled in ads and dressed to impress in lyrics. Made to fit many hands and yours slipped in and gripped it as you fired intestines with what you thought your only life was.

And I feel sorry for you, because to you that gun may seem like it's on your side until somebody takes out and turns it on you.

Starving

We are starving for freedom. Waiting for the chains
on our throats to be fractured,the lock locking the
mouth in a tongue twister to be swallowed, our
intestines reach for limitless visions to feed them,
for colors to shade what has been translucent for too
long, to solve the puzzles seen in pupils, save a
mind before it's lynching, the stench of bars lingers
in frail noses. Carved not deep enough the letters f-
r-e-e, it was never felt. We arc starving. Starving for
freedom.

Untitled

Rolling down cracked windows is rain. Rain that
resembles tears soaking bed sheets of a little kid.

Who doesn't know what happiness looks like, he
never sees it in a mirror, only shattered dreams
crusted in the reflection, shattered and limping like
the way of his legs because his friends told him that
was real, real like the tears he faces when he sees
that daddy is gone.

Young in a world that would mature him before his
body and mind could handle it, having to make art
of toxic paints he stroked images of black and blue
abuse and red anger on his portrait, looking for
beauty but in the cracks of rainbows he couldn't
find it.

Not a slither, a portion, his life was puzzles so how
could he piece together a piece from an artist's eyes,
stroke something of his history,
when time wouldn't even hand him the brush to
stroke future

The child with the notebook

Sitting in a corner his thoughts call
home,crusted,dented and dark but the glow he
plants in his eyes could blossom happiness.Just a
child.

Small enough to have his silhoutte be crushed to
crumbs by the greedy hands of the outside, so he
has a notebook.
With lines shorter than his history but he fits it in.
Fitting in times where he had to fill shoes he
couldn't fit when believers became shadows.

Imprint the struggle he holds at the tip of led pens
too organic to copy and paste, the pain became
words that reflected his image like a mirror but
mirrors hold you and he didn't see him.
He saw his fractured dreams on cold floors, he saw
a boy trying to be man but a father's words or
rapper's verse didn't teach him so he learned
artificial, by the sagging pants infecting a street like
syphilis.

He constructed words like pyramids, words like
buildings, he touched skies long before his fingers

could he tattooed paper with ink ,by the way his body was dented and twisted I knew he was holding something that his body couldn't pick up any longer.

I notice the concentration by the lines in his forehead, the sweat back stroking off, the innocence in his smiles. Hands get sore and peel but he writes. A story in his young mind ready to battle, ready to win.

Smile

Today, I decided to smile.

Through the black and blue memories I hold like
infants in cold coated brain cells, the lips worked
like geometry, curving in the angle of sunshines,
bent and tattooed, I wear smiles like they're
permanent.

Pierce through hurt and cowardness using the glow
I wear in dimples to clothe shadows. Cracking the
bars blooming from the throat that burned in the
esophagus the smell of steel instilled in me at a
young age was the fear that showers would drown
my dreams before those images could drench
reality.

But today, I found that shape, settling in the spot by
cheekbones, birthed in buried teeth,unwinding the
dreadlock of a tongue I held that was twisted in a
rainbow of taste buds for too long. Today I decided
to smile.

Smile with me.

Trigger

On that day, she decided to pull the trigger, bare the
shell cases of blooming though her body had barely
grown, but she wore it like addiction.

Piercing her peer's normalcy on her, breaking
innocence, blowing holes through the doors that
kept her from becoming the massacre so many girls
become a part of.
On that day the loaded forever was in her hand,
buried in index, caressed by thumbs.
She heard the whispers secreting through sinister
winds telling her to pull, so she did, finding cold
comfort in potent shadows.

Numb. Blasting through her thoughts the printed
ammo carving a story on brain cells secreting
memory. Through the pain and pleasure of the
trigger, you see a little girl.

With pants releasing from her temple finding
comfort on the floor, she looks in the eyes of a guy
she barely knows, baring virginity in the zip locked
legs of confusion.

But that day she made the decision. Sexual pleasure
covering retinas made her lose the battle

She pulled the trigger

Introduction of Destruction

Hello. My name is Alcohol.

And I am here to bring hell. Infringe families like broken bones, my liquid is meant to lick your gut ,shackle your pride , poison your throat I ooze through warm tissue like arctic love but my destruction is far from cold, I burn.

Like your conscious is being set to flames I torch, turn your eyes acrylic your retains sit translucent. With an oven of a mind, your tickled soul playing tricks on you, I am there.

To be that shadow you can't escape, lately I've been mixed with fun and kids but that doesn't make me less potent, I strike, with tempting lyrics humming off my body, my mouth, the place every person seems to love kissing, making love to government-made craft, bruising my rim with the staining outlines of lips I work like magic.

Before your body has a chance to think I'm moving you, I bare destruction wrapping around you, wrapping around your skull making you a slave to

29

your own thoughts, I cover you with the known aroma of addiction and parties, your mouth lingering with the tinted canvas of my silhouette, I made your innocence leak ,bleed through the fingers gripping me like a newborn it laid deceased on my glass, I was made for this.

Born in the toxic labs of pain, I was never meant to love you I harm you and starve you. Sit in colorful designs but leech on you because this is what the government told me to do. To never smile at you, I sink you, melting in the pools of my missiles. I can't wait for the day you have to live off me, with life crusting on your tongue and me on your side, I will laugh. And my laughs will be heard, biting through your eardrums, but too numb to really be absorbed. I am known for killing millions, aborting your lives before your time, I am here to kill you. So nice to meet you. I really hope we meet again.

Unrecognizable

Would my ancestors recognize this place?

Of foreign material, stroking normal in our minds,
would they understand, the n word vibrating off
wet tongues like pools, putting chains back on
ankles, back on eyes sculpted into the outline of our
brain cells like a pen marking us back into the past,
would they know us?

With pants sagging lower than lost souls, lower
than pavement connecting us, would they know the
movement of young girl's bodies, with back sides
facing a blinking light the umbilical cord to media,
never hesitant to show the world their abilities,
lynching their skin in skirts and shirts because
they're told cellulite is to be laughed at, buried in
acceptance so they hide it, behind fabric that barely
covers them , barely existent to a body who isn't
loved anymore it is constructed.

Would my ancestors recognize this place? Of
extinct pride in the color of our skin, everyone
wants be mixed with European. Knowing that the

paler they are, the more people will accept and they just wanna be the best so they would do anything.

They would allow their life to be more translucent ,invisible ,like the the visions of daddies in a child's home, battered like the fish cooking in the kitchen but this will not be tasty, this will sting.

Would my ancestors notice the poison that swim in our eyes, letting currency murder us slowly, we depend on money to love us not knowing that us adding cash is just subtracting reality so what's really the income. But for proceeds we proceed and it's sad to see, that our ancestors worked hours in cotton and grass to get cash and when you get some you go crazy for Jordan's killing each other for human made labels, would my ancestors believe it?

That once when they were labeled they were sliced, punctured and penetrated and now that we're addicts to the newest fashion we're becoming a label again it's just remixed but the same deadly song humming through our bones, would my ancestors accept this?

I'm just hoping that my smile, eyes, skin will ring some sort of memory to them. Because this world I live in is too unfamiliar for me to even remember what it looks like normally.

News

Breaking News! Breaking News!

A police officer once again has shot an innocent
Black man. Well, they say his gun accidentally went
off he didn't mean to do it, he just saw a man of
what he calls foreign complexion with a roll of
money in his pocket, and his instinct told him that
couldn't be his.

He judged him by the skin painted on him, the car
he drove. Never did he know this man had 3
daughters back at home, waiting for him at the
dinner table, but his food would sit there cold.
Frozen like that night,Christmas Eve, with a man
waiting for the birth of sun the next day but loud
pops would abort it while, he laid a stump.Burying
his blood in pavement's cracks, he was vacuumed
of life, this cop never did care.

His people had been on bills for many years, his
grandparents had backyards full of black kids being
more of an adult they could ever be, he knew that
America would be on his side. On his side like a

gun he pointed, pulled out a potent mother of crying slugs, he fired.

Frying the wind as it glided piling in ligaments, it scorched. Like oil hitting a pan, it sizzled, baring the white tissue inside of him. As his girls waited at home, with a big tree and presents with daddy written across them, a wife in bed waiting for her husband to be beside her, she didn't know, that his side of the bed would become a stone, erect and old, she would soon know that a crooked cop's pistol made him feel manly, made him feel like he could be somebody with a gun resting in his thumbs, he wrote in the darkness, scribbled in a body the ink of tombstones, he made a novel with bullets.

The police have said they are investigating. But what's to be investigated about a life taken just because he couldn't choose what shade God had painted on his body, what was to be looked at? A coward cop with holes he wore in his soul, put deeper holes inside of thighs and the chest, and don't tell me you didn't see the smirk on his face as my human race is becoming extinct from shell cases.

My baby! My baby! is all his mother could say. Her mouth was wide like the caves in her son's stomach, she cried. Tears filling up his T-shirt, wetting his now cold body. I want to hold that mother. The mother of Oscar Grant, Trayvon Martin, Sean Bell, Courtney Mathis,Adam Wheeler,Timothy Thomas and a hundred more black boys, I want to hold their mothers. As another life becomes a haunting article, I pray for them and I ask you.
Is this really breaking news? Or another daily routine?

Untitled

That day, he ripened.

His days of growing as a stitch into shadows faded from his skin, he was known as the forbidden fruit of his streets, mind bruised like apples, images he carried rotting in fingernails but finally his body blossomed, sprouting fragile seeds that changed him from a boy into a man.

This soil he walked on was no longer potent. With every step he made fertilization, filling the ground with new hope, birthing from years of being withered.

He ripened like the look in his mother's eyes when seeing him smile, like his city in the sunshine being the only make-up it needs to be beautiful, he ripened. Breaking loose of block's thrones, the stinging feeling he encountered on his fingers, pounding like bee stings on his palms he unwrapped, left bare and nude for life to construct and he was built.

Like nature hugged his eyes, his pupils were penetrated with roses, drowning in veins were gardens grown by the warmth of his words loaded in his throat, darkness was behind him, buried in his pockets swallowed by the seam, he no longer had the thundering words of loneliness tattooed on his thoughts. He sits there, with a glow he can barely hide leaking from his lips spreading into his cheeks, I look at him, and all i can do is smile.

Because to see a stone turn into a diamond is something more magical than magic itself.

Bus stop

We're at that bus stop.

Not really knowing where we're going but we let
the roads lead us. Let the corners caress our skin
and shade feelings in us, we let the rain bathe us
like we were starving for it's beauty, we loved the
way it drenched us.

We let the air carve us with it's slipping silhouette,
dent us with it's crisp touch, swallow in the depths
of blood vessels, twirl in the neverending braid of
our stomach clothe in the dresses of our tissue, we
were there.

Waiting for that bus to take us through roars and
chirps in this concrete jungle we live in, to be held
captive by the waving hands of the trees and the
pure perfection lingering from roses, we sat in the
seats, eyes opened like arms ready to hug any vision
keep it in our minds and never let it go.
We wait for this adventure, with courage held in
our hands and adrenaline constructing in our feet,
we let this ride take us where our body couldn't.

Cold

It was cold. Like the forgotten clothes in a closet,
buried away to be dust, it was cold.

Like arctic whispers were tattooed in our ear canals,
like the snow outlined our lips,

our eyes felt frozen into one image repeating in the
cracks of our skull making memory, sunk into our
bones, it was cold.

Like Christmas greeted us right in the face, tickling
our jaw line, our cheeks shivered, our words ran
into the cave of our throats, it was cold.

Like shelter has forgotten us, lingering from our
skin the erect smells of cold creating perfume in our
noses, it was cold.

And I will always remember that feeling.

Bury

I'm searching.

For a place to bury past, that is seeping through my
eyes like a faucet, revealing my soul. A place to rest
it in soil, to cut it of its moaning voice like a drum
slowly slipping away from its beat.

That is running circles in my dreams remixing
reality, making a brick in the tissue of my skin, can
you feel it?

Hard and erect, it lives in me.
Sealed with the shadow's kisses giving it pleasure,
it leaks. A liquid like syrup making my skin sticky
and sinking and coated with the colors of past
making rainbows burst through me, I bleed them,
they taste like hell's meals finding way to my
mouth,

spinning like a spiral in battered taste buds, they
hold me captive in the whispers of their translucent
bars, they are there to tease me, beat me forever, in
my mind.

41

I am here to bury them. Remove the tattoos that swallowed my existence.

Numb3rs

February 16, 1998.

Before I could even burst a cry from immature
lungs, I was a number.

Lucid digits leaked on fresh skin, my scent was
belonging to the government's noses, they raised
me. My mind babysat by the media on a daily,
raised by the false articles and news stories coating
TV screens, by pixels penetrating pavements
scripting the streets we live in, I was a number.

Like a leech they were there. To hang from my
throat and control the words thundering inside me,
freedom of speech is a myth.

A myth like our song claiming we are the home of
the brave when we rape, take and kill and walk
away with smiles so how can you stain the word
brave on our flag when our eyes leak the past blood
drips we sliced from silhouettes, from crying
mothers and their babies killed in cribs they gripped
on their teddy bears, their only friends, humming
their last goodbye.

43

I was a number in schools, they wanted to drain my skull of education, I was a kid guilty of being black never sorry if my only crime is survival, it is an instinct.

I held a number clothed and sinking in eyelids so every time I slept I was reminded that this land was my lease.

And the truth is we are all numbers. Non-believers will never learn, they will be fried of thoughts till thoughts burn and are foreign. In my mind I have a question, "Would the government care if I was killed". And I'm not sure I would get an answer.

Happiness

The story of happiness. Clothed in fresh smiles and
yellows, it is brought to us. In our eyes, we hold the
seeds of its blossoms. The lips
of its kisses. We wait for them to be birthed in our
lives, decaying the hurt that kept us buried

Wrapped

I was that package.

Delivered at pavement's cracks, wrapped with the
skin of the skies bruising me with leaking delicacy
of the clouds and the screams of the sun, tightly
coiled and curled like a fetus, I already had a
nickname;

The stunted arrival, aborted box, I was looked down
at and expected to tear like the inner thoughts of
battered women leaching to bathroom tiles,
knowing the number of them like the back of her
hand , or the back of his hand you can say.

I was the voice of a million whispers spun together
in erotic waves of fabric clothed on my lungs, I
breathe thunder, vibrating off brittle buildings
caught in the tangles of the bricks like a young
girl's hair, young like my visions barely splashed in
the pools of my cranium but the images i pieced in
pupils were meant to end this stretched drought, to
stab the hunger of wanting more.

My mind grumbled as I walked this world reaching for what could not be explained, I was the package that could not understood. Dressed with beauty licking the mind but my beauty was fresh, straight out of the bristles in God's paintbrush I glowed like the sun had been painted into my tissue I was bright like neon never did I create darkness with placed footsteps, I was rough around the edges, I peeled perfection's paint revealing my mistakes but I allowed them to be bare. And rain had gotten to me, sinking me in a new sort reality.

So, I'm telling you to reveal me. The package. And realize that being wrapped up can't protect us from everything.

Woman

The woman in the jacket covered in the paint of
shadows, glasses burying eyes into carved plastic,
her fingers told a story of past loves and screw
you's carved and so visible her heart hanging by
loose screws and nails passion was falling into her
stomach digested like she never needed it.

Her cheeks swelled like the sky in the early
mornings it swelled like it was crammed with
laughter, but it was stuck somewhere along the road
to her lips, it wouldn't leave her.

She was the color of wonders, she had the hum of
questions fuming from her skull, dancing
somewhere in between the shoulders of the winds,
her tongue creaked with dehydrated words moaning
in her bones, throat dyed with the patterns of
past,having a hard time fading

I could read her just by looking at her. Not knowing
her full novel, but she revealed a chapter of herself,
never even having to say anything, a pure print I
found in her.

Picture This

Picture this. A park, clothed by the trees, with the flowers humming rainbows from its tongue, the whispers we hold in our fingernails, the smell of birth tattooing smiles into the waters of our cheekbones. Picture this. A bench that's been sat on by the lonely, depressed, it's bent, acute nowhere near the tearing inside of a person split like their heart they harvest pain in their stomach stretching out like crooked roots and twisting their spine they walk with burdens

I write

I write because life is complicated

So fingers kissing paper like a lover's lips are the best feeling. When my tales are crammed on canvases, it makes me smile, filling up lines with oceans.

My mouth never has to move because paper is my voice, so I leave the speech to its lips. Leave the spit to fly from its tongue crafted in a notebook and dripping like a faucet.

I write because these bars box with the skies battering clouds into black and blues, write because seeing pain die is the most beautiful decay I have ever witnessed, writing to add a tint of color to this black and white world we live in.

Can't you see my paper crying? Secreting the tears my body was too scared to release, smiling to me just to show that I am still an innocent child in this adult world.

So swallow a piece of my puzzled life, that is torn
and built with stones, but still worth it all.

Battered Yet Beautiful

Mommy's wallet. Sitting on a crusted dresser, crammed with the complex's cobwebs. Holding bills going to calm the tummy's of her little toddlers.

Crowded with a couple foreclosure notes and some dreams she sat and wrote, forming imagination in her frontal lobe turning in an art from her artistic eyeballs, blinking up masterpieces.

She sometimes shares conversations with nighttime skies, carves the moon with her frail fingernails, penetrating her frustration into the rocks.

Her wallet, becoming as blank as the walls. Dusty internally because happiness was never birthed there, it holds mommy's past worries.

Crumbled light bills live in it, tears age in the fabric molding and leaving a stench.

When she goes home, she is comforted by the toxic aromas of Hennessy with the urban sirens her music.

She is a battered yet beautiful. And though she doesn't know this, a glow can be seen from her bruises.

Portrait

He created her portrait. His hands made strokes of dark blues and blacks under her eyes. He splattered violets on the tip of her bottom lip popped pupils with seeping red blood staining the face from eyes to the jaw line.

This woman was getting painted and his frustrated hands were the painter, leaking abusive paint from his knuckles he finger painted blue under eyes of someone a depressing gray.

She thought. About all these cut and bruises that he paints and she hasn't seen God in days, she whispers his name, too scared and tired to scream.

When he's drunk, she becomes his canvas. He continues to pound and her face drowns all the colors of the rainbow.

Continuing to hit and hit her until her face turns a color he has never seen. A shade of translucent, he realizes, this is the color of expiration.

And no matter how many times he tries to paint her back to beauty, back out of the rich golden gates of heaven, back to cherry red their love used to be, back to her chocolate covered skin, her sweet piglet pink lips as much as he wants to take her out of the blue skies with her white glowing robe and halo, he can't

He can't paint this. He got addicted to painting his whole home with hands and forgot,

only God's hands are big enough to paint life.

Untitled

I am a woman's butt. Imprinted by the hands of
men with lips licking.

I am a drug to some, leave pupils consuming then
needing a higher dosage. I am the thing that
repeatedly intoxicates the mind, I absorb the curses
stretched onto horny faces grown onto women and
used as a tool to make love to fingertips

A man's temptation in motion, soaked in rap's
stereotypes, viciously sliced at by hurtful words,
painfully penetrated wit lies dripping from mouths,
I cannot be hidden

My curve is put into a light and advertised. I am
told I need to be big to be accepted, I am told I need
to be big to be gripped by dark, dirty sexual palms
that caress what we are told to expose into a world
that beats me when it sees me, believe these bruises
I am in pain.

Battered by the grasp of overly attached hands. I
was made famous by the names of sin sticking to
woman's rear ends, donk. tush, derier, they don't

care women are scared to bare these words on
manipulated skin.

It's sad to see instead of reaching for her brain, you
reach much much lower to greet me, the thing you
see greater than what's inside her mind, these
women see something so blurry, also barely able to
connect the pixels of the portrait and see an image

I have become the strongest thing in the sketch of a
woman, I seep through the tiny cracks of real love
and turned artificial.
These are the words of whispers. Already louder
than ever in the media.

Nights

The night we went out.

Drenched by the rainbows of city lights, our minds were nude, crafted by cold winds and cracked concretes, we dreamt of sugar coated stars and got the chance to draw the galaxies , outlining canvases.

Cars flashed by us like stale memories barely able to be wrapped and protected by eyelids, our eyes lit like New ports because something ignited when we finally held hands. Like a million soaked symphonies stringing together I love you's were bathing our fingers, we pawned our feelings into each other's young souls.

We sold our hearts to each other's lips the moment they sewed beauty into us, I would sit and count our stares, we would sit for minutes , capturing the depths of each other's insides and saving those portraits.

That night changed you. To think when I met you ,you only had 3 hairs stroked above your upper lip, you were still a little boy. We grew like dancing daisies in grandma's gardens, with a rhythm like no other.

A dark and cold silhouette of our city, we spun gold into our smiles, feeling rich with empty pockets.

We walked the roads less traveled, scraping our moments on the same streets that raised our love.

Twisted World

Her world is a world of lipsticks, tight fabrics and cracked reflections.

Reflecting a girl, bruised by expectations, seeping into her throat, she holds cobwebs in every word she speaks. Clicking like thunder birthed in skies is her heels, lynching curbs, swallowing money in the waters of drenched pockets.

So scared that if she doesn't meet perfection her image will sink, drowning like her tears in white pillowcases, molding the scent of altered beauty, blooming from her brain of puzzles and crosswords, she crosses her legs, trying to hide lust sessions in black jeeps, to cover adventures in freezing alleyways when she just needed someone to be there.

When evil printed girl's bodies with "For Sale" and her calls to God went to voicemail she was held, by artificial hugs with street winds locking her in with pavement whispers, her soul leaked like a faucet never tightly screwed and her mind was filled with the images of dilapidated daisies and scrambled skies.

She will never remember the little girl she was, with little dresses and little dreams. She grew to bruise with all the colors of struggle, she spends hours to confuse herself into being someone else, into being a stranger she has never known, but her mirror tells her this is you and you have to accept it.

So with sweat dripping, a face connected into her puzzles and her mind, she clothes in a black hole millions of girls face.

And all I can really do is pray for her.

About the Author

Leija Farr is an author from Seattle, WA. She has always had a passion for writing poems and loved to hear about upcoming open mics and talent shows. She is 15 years old and a sophomore attending Cleveland High School. She hopes to attend Howard University when she is older and become a Broadcast Journalist. This is her first book of poetry. She plans to write many more.

About Young Urban Authors

Young Urban Authors has a mission to empower young adults by equipping them with the necessary tools that can lead to rewarding careers as entrepreneurs, through appreciation of the literary arts and the knowledge of available opportunities to publish their own literary work. At-risk youth are targeted for program recruitment, such as delinquents, dropouts, pregnant teens, etc; however, the program is also open to non at-risk youth. The purpose is to collectively empower residential youth seeking sustainable skills and careers that the publishing arts have to offer.

Here is Your Chance to Support a Great Youth Organization!

The Young Urban Authors Project is thrilled to announce that 15 of the youth in our program have become published authors. These young people currently have books selling on our website as well as large online book retailers. We are so proud of their accomplishments, and want to continue providing this same opportunity to other youth in the community.

Word of our program has spread throughout the community. We now have a waiting list of young people who would like to take part in the program during the winter and spring quarter. In order to continue our mission, and make this a reality for those youth, we really need your help.

Our goal is to serve 20 youth per year. Some of these young people would not have an opportunity to achieve this on their own, nor would they have the tools to do so. Please help us reach our goal of serving 20 young people per year.

Your donation is tax deductible, and we appreciate whatever you can give. Know that you are helping to empower our youth and provide a brighter future in today's world. We partnered with the Seattle Neighborhood Group in our efforts to (develop) and expand our program, providing more youth with a chance to be heard.

Checks should be made payable to, "Young Urban Authors". If you prefer to donate online, please go to our website: www.youngurbanauthors.org.

There is no better feeling then knowing you have helped a child. If you have any questions, suggestions, or comments about the Young Urban Author Project, please contact us.

Frankie Roe

Young Urban Authors

1810 E. Yesler

Seattle, WA 98122

Seattle Youth Violence Prevention Initiative

The Seattle Youth Violence Prevention Initiative (SYVPI) tackles the issue of youth violence with an approach that incorporates evidenced-based strategies along with home-grown, youth-and community-created programs. The goals of the Initiative are to achieve a 50% reduction in juvenile court referrals for violence and a 50% reduction in suspensions and expulsions from selected middle schools due to violence-related incidents.

The Initiative funds some of these home-grown programs through Community Matching Grants. These programs supplement existing Initiative services by providing positive, healthy activities that support a safe, non-violent lifestyle. The Young Urban Authors' Project is one of the first grantees under the Community Matching Grant program. It helps to fulfill the mission of the Initiative by assisting our youth to find and share their voices through the written word.

Other Titles

Leading Thru Change – Standing Above the Crowd by Amina Mohammed

Long Way Down by Tajh'Nique Richardson

My Cry Out – The Story of My Tears by April Wilburn

Blasian Drive – Having the Determination to Continue by Shalena Duong

Life As It Is by Jennifer Gutierrez

The Journey of a Solid Soldier by Jimmy Phin

Hi Drama – A Collection of Short Stories by Karlina Khorn

A Walk Down Memory Lane by Monique Blockman

Wrote This Because of You by CurDesia' Hudson

Young Life by Hanan Soulaiman

Flipped by Yazmine Mobley

Stuck in this world All Alone by Alrick Hollingsworth

Standing Alone – A mini collection of short stories by Mattie Alexander

Found – A journey to Salvation by Tayonna Gault

A letter to my Grandma by Kylea Spears

Loyalty then Love by Takeysha King

The me They don't See by Alexis Tobar

End of the Road by Tasha Barnes

Chosen One by Theo Thomas

Free by Kaeliah Haynes

What Lies Beneath Her by Cindy Villavicencio

Perception by Jelia Farr